The Mind of a Romantic
Elena Zubanov
Kristina Puzin

Author's Note

My name is Elena, and I'm the creator and writer behind this wonderful book of inspirational poems. I thank you for having my book in your precious hands. In my heart, I wish that my creation will impact your life one way or another. Writing, to me, is a magical haven where I go with my thoughts, desires, ideas, and hopes. When writing, I close my eyes and go to a space where I can be myself, imagining the world I'd like to belong to—a place that no one has stepped into yet. This place in my mind is so pure and unforgettable that I can come and revisit it as many times as I want.

Now, I'd like you to close your eyes and imagine yourself in a space where all of your worries and struggles are diminished for a moment. Perhaps you may be compelled to revisit the most meaningful events of your life. Don't be afraid to do so—jump in wholeheartedly.

I hope this book, which you found on a shelf at your local store, will somehow help you understand that we, as human beings, are very passionate, sensitive, creative, and delicate individuals. I hope you'll understand that it's okay to love and be loved. To grieve for someone. To let go of the love of your life. To love and struggle. To forgive and forget. To have deep wishes that lift your spirit to a level of unbelievable happiness.

Trust me, it's alright.

Welcome to " The Mind of a Romantic."

Step Into the Heart of the Words.
This book holds more than pages—it holds a journey.
It's a doorway into a world where poetry breathes.

On this page, you'll find a single QR code
that unlocks poetic journeys—
brought to life through voice, imagery, and emotion.
It's simple to scan, unforgettable to feel.

Let your heart lead the way.
Scan. Watch. Feel. Remember.

To access each journey:
Open your phone's camera and point it at the QR code.
Tap the link that appears—and let the dream begin.

Written and dreamed by Elena Zubanov
"Where emotion meets imagination, poetry awakens."

Dear reader,
You are never too grown
to dream.

Table of Contents

I See

The alignment of the stars
Was meant only for the two of us.
Every moment with you
Is like an explosion of something new.

My eyes see only you,
They tend to love everything about you.

My lips have learned the taste of your compassion,
And now I'll be the one who gets your passion.

Your touch,
Helped me heal from every mistreat and such.

I feel your soul, I feel your spirit,
I feel the colors of your mood,
I know you are longing to be understood.

A Thought

What is love?
Is it something I can't live without?
Is it something I can't breathe without?
Do I get it from a special source?
Or is it an illusion about to burst?
Shall I compare it with a pretty rose—
Red, but the thorns are very exposed.
It's nice to look at,
But once you take it in your hand,
Its thorns so sharp,
They can hurt you,
And you'll bleed a lot.
Then you'll ask yourself,
Was it worth picking up?
Was the beauty of a red rose a delusion?
I'm thinking to myself,
Maybe I should have settled down
With a less powerful flower.
That way, my heart would be calm.
Perhaps it's a very easy way out—
To choose something simple
And not fight or find more about.

A Prayer

I'd like to open the unknown door to your soul,
To find that special key in whole.

Into your inner world of ups and downs,
To where black and white bounce.

I'd like to hug every sadness you swallow,
Give instead laughter you never follow.

I'd like to wipe every diamond tear of yours with the softest handkerchief.
And give every reason for you to achieve.

Everything that you desire,
All that you admire.

For visions of yours to be transcribed,
And become unbelievably revived.

Drown

I felt connected to him,
Totally drowning on a whim.
His gaze went through my soul,
Till I totally forgot it all.

Forgot every pain I endured,
Forgot every word spoken at me,
That abused only me.
Every tear that I shed,
With a huge regret.

And then it happened again...

Tears are coming down like rain,
They are beautifully precious,
A river with bitter confessions.

Have you ever felt stabbed in your soul?
Have you ever felt every emotion out of control?
Have you ever felt a connection was broken?
Now nothing can ever be spoken?

Every word he said,
Still in the back of my head.
Was it all a lie?
I don't think I want a reply.

Blur

Have you ever thought
About the person next to you?
Who says good night,
But silences what may be true.

This person is beautiful,
In their own way.
But for some reason,
They're drifting by the day.

That familiar smile,
Fading with time.
Their voice growing quieter,
Failing to seem fine.

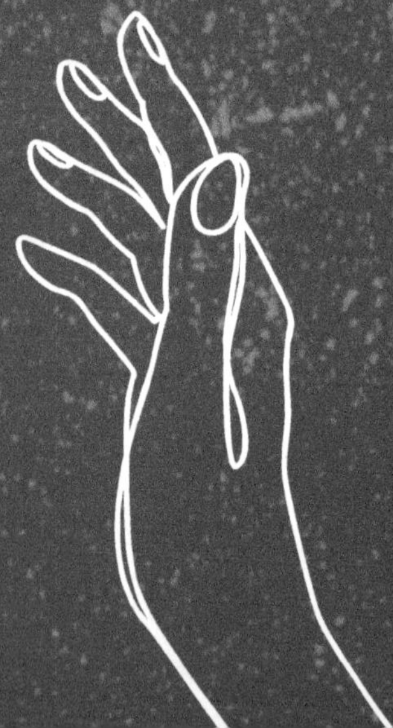

Intimacy

I want to feel your world—
Unpleasant, righteous, or very twirled.
I'm yearning for your attention,
I'd like to be in your dimension.

Please, fill me in with your emotions,
Please, hug me tight with your distortions.
I'd like to know your darker side,
And learn your brighter, if you don't mind.

Please, wrap around me—
Your mighty hands and let me be.
Look at me with your eyes closed,
And yet, I'll feel your gaze... and be content,
I suppose.

Evening Wonder

Love and sexual desires,
Is it all that she requires?
To feel special inside,
And feel like a lady of the night?

I ask myself,
What makes me happy and fulfilled?
What makes my heart and soul
Feel it all?
Is it a man who stands by me,
With his love and affection beside me?
Whose touches are warm and exciting,
Whose voice is warm and inviting?

Is it a man who makes me feel like a queen,
A queen whose days are magical and dear?
A queen whose negative thoughts will disappear,
A queen whose life will be a total dream?

Is it a man in whose arms she'll melt,
A man who finds her face angelic,
Her body beside him an ancient relic?

Is it a man who sees her for who she is,
With all her troubles and sins?

Is it a man who loves me with all he has,
Because he knows a remedy for my distress?

One day I'd like to meet you in your dream,
And take that journey to the extreme.
I want to see into your soul,
My goodness, O, how I'm yearning to feel it all.

I want to see the colors of your mood,
I want to be with you in a place where prayers
Can be heard and understood.
I want to feel your energy that flows through
Your blood stream,
O, how I wish to be a good part of your dream.

I want to travel within you.
I want to hear the music you listen to.

I want to float in your soul,
And learn the basic nature of your core.

The Pulse

There's a rhythm in everything around you—
It makes this world so unique and just for you.
Rhythm when tiny rain drops lay softly on your
Eyelash,
Rhythm in a generous wind brush.

When sun rays dance on your cheeks,
When snowflakes land on your lips.
When you watch a hummingbird,
Whose beats of wings vary,
And are just extraordinary.

When you immerse your feet in ocean deep,
As water keeps rushing,
While you keep blushing.
When you stand next to a waterfall—
Witnessing its beauty and counting each fall.

When you hear the sound of music,
Each note piercing through your heart and soul,
And nothing can stop you—
From achieving big dreams at all.

Party for One

I want to celebrate me today,
Give a shoutout clear as a piercing sunray.

I want to say wonderful words to myself for being
there,
Listening intently everywhere.

I want to rejoice,
Because I have a beautiful voice.

I want to thank my creator for giving me a beautiful
body,
So I can be a gift to somebody.

I want to thank him for giving me wings to fly,
It doesn't come easy to get up and not die.

I want to give thanks for my precious soul,
Since that's what makes me completely whole.

Blessing

What a magnificent morning to start your day,
But you will say it's just ordinary,
Yet I think it's quite the contrary.

Open your inner eyes,
And you'll be in a beautiful paradise.
Heaven of love, beauty, imagination,
Only of your pure creation.

You'll be satisfied
With every little detail
That you have in your
mind.

Look up to see the baby blue sky,
With beautiful clouds floating up high.
Perhaps it's about to rain—
So what?
Everything is wonderful in its own
way.

Amidst The Crowd

Can you make love to me,
Without even touching me?

Can you speak to me,
And grab my attention,
Without a single word to mention?

Can you feel the taste of my kiss?
Can you tell that you'll miss
My presence in your life?

Because the energy we share,
Is so wonderful and rare.

Can you see my soul,
And be at peace with it all?

The Ember

How did it happen to me?
What was the reason behind it all?
Why didn't I experience that before?

When I looked into his eyes,
I saw a glimpse of something nice.

Something that gave me warmth and peace,
Something that brought my mind to ease.

Perhaps in the moment I understood,
How a love language can feel so good.

Perhaps all it takes,
Is finding someone with the same mistakes.

It seems like I've missed a lot in my life,
Something that makes me come alive,

Something that can make my blood boil,
To the degree I'd feel amazingly royal.

Let's spread our wings,
Soar as high as we can.

Say hello to a new start,
Even if we are far apart.
We'll dissolve all negativity,
With beautiful possibility.

Him

I picture a field of flowers,
A gentle wind will brush them,
With generosity that follows.

I picture a sunny day,
One that would feel to me
Like a holiday.

Because you'll put your arms around me,
And whisper gently
How you feel about me.

Your voice will soothe my soul,
Like healing medicine, overall.

Hooked

Let me see your face,
Let me catch your gaze.

Allow me access to your heart—
So that we may never part.

Your body is an open door,
Welcoming holy water down my core.

Please share the gifts that you possess—
Love and kindness are my guess.

I want to look into your eyes,
And see a glimpse of paradise.

Where Love and goodness conquer all—
O God, have mercy as I fall.

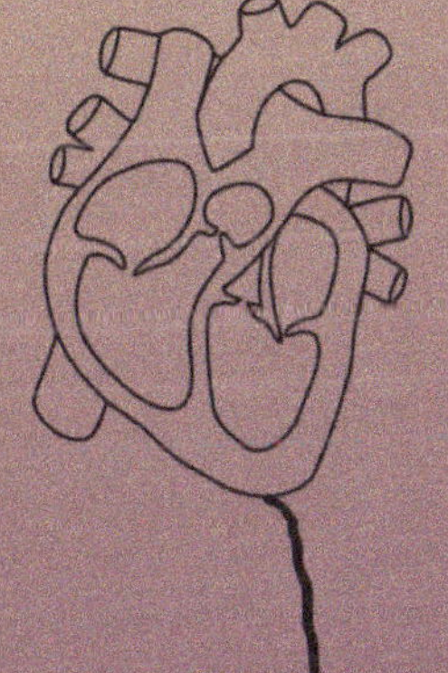

Taste

Can you feel the taste of love?
Can you understand its meaning,
And the depth of love's beginning?

How magical to have it underneath your core—
And learn never to ignore.
Just give it a sweet hug—
And embrace it just like that.

Look straight into its eyes,
You'll feel complete peace,
And learn how wonderful it is.

So take its hand,
And hold on with trust
Until the very end.

While I'm Awake

I often wonder what truly awaits me on the other side—
When will my last heartbeat decide?

Will I be lost in the tunnel of light,
Or perhaps darkness swallows me with its delight?

Will I be strong enough,
And act tough?
Or will I choose to cry,
And pretend that I didn't die?

Will I see someone's face at the end of my tunnel,
Calling my name as if it were on a television channel?

Will I be greeted as a wanted guest,
Or would I feel like an outcast?

Wake Up

Look around you and see the beauty of this world—
Even though sometimes it can be so cold.

Have you ever tried to taste a rain drop?
Have you ever tried to see?
No, really see and feel—
That everything around you, my dear,
Is very real.

The wind brushes against your skin,
The ocean water is blue and clean,
The grains of sand are radiant with gold,
They never allow you to get cold.

The sun goddess is so generous to us,
She sends her golden rays
To the ungrateful human race.

Rest Easy Reader

When I need to rest my soul,
I go to a place with no worries to patrol.

I see a crystal-blue, peaceful lake,
Water flowing like there's nothing at stake.

I see luscious, green grass,
A gorgeous white horse among the mass.

She stands waiting for me,
Radiant to finally be free.

Waiting for me to give her attention,
To welcome her properly to my mansion.

Rupture

When I start to think about my deep desires,
It makes my body and soul,
Fight like never before.

When the angel of darkness takes control,
O, how I'd like to immerse myself into it all—
The world with no boundaries,
The world with no laws,
The world with a total chaos.

But then the angel of light
Comes to me in a beautiful delight,
And whispers to me:
"Perhaps you should rethink it all
For the sake of your soul."

Melt

Have you ever felt broken, sad and cold,
Until it's time to get old?
Have you ever felt like there are no more doors to open,
Because everything seems so broken?

The pain inside, like a poison,
Doesn't want to show me the signs of hope.
It's killing me without sweet mercy,
I'm drifting away,
I'm flying away,
To the darkest colors of array.

My soul is slowly fading in the dark,
I'm afraid I will lose it completely,
Without giving to it a sweet hug.

I don't want to be empty or sad,
I want my creator to help me not feel so bad.

I want my soul to shine again,
I want to stand tall,
And rise beneath it all.

Wisher

Everywhere I look,
I choose to see beauty and light.
I say no to darkness,
Turn away from what is not so bright.

I wish every pain
Would be a conclusion
Of some misunderstood illusion.

I wish every love story
Would be an enchanted tale,
Where I'm the main character,
Destined to prevail.

Every smile
That I have seen,
I'd like to put in my pocket,
And give them away
To someone who shouldn't cr
Anyway.

Every positive thought
That flies in the air,
I want to catch
And keep forever.

Listen Dear

Not everyone can hear the sound of music,
Perhaps not everyone has the ability to listen—
To follow their heart,
Because they're used to the ordinary beat,
The one that doesn't give your heart a special heat.

I often think about musicians all around the world—
How they give wings of hope,
How they are match makers with their note.

With their profound sound and lyrics that cut down to your heart,
Giving your soul a complete makeover,
The kind that gives you goosebumps all over.

The Gift

You can create a world with your imagination,
Where you can play a lead role of your creation.

The world where everything is so outstanding,
The world without pain and misunderstanding.

The world where you can see a sunset,
And be so happy within your mindset.

The world where oceans are so deep,
And yet the fear of drowning
Wouldn't even be near,
Because the sound of broken waves
Is all you would try to embrace.

The world where colors are so bright,
You'd be afraid to go blind.

The world where flower's aroma,
Will get you so high,
Perhaps you'll understand the meaning
Of what it takes to fly.

Tailored to Perfection

Who am I ?
You would ask me.
What am I?
You would question me.
Am I just this body?
Am I somebody?

What's beneath this beautiful female suit?
Will I ever be understood?
What if I tell you,
I'm like a deep blue ocean,
Full of emotion.
I'm filled with a lot of power and love,
I'm someone who has a good heart and can laugh.
My eyes are the perfect door to my spirit and soul,
All you have to do is look and you'll see it all.

I Am You

I wonder, why do people think they have a right?
To put someone down and decide
That white skin color
Dominates a beautiful chocolate one.

We all have the same spirit and soul,
And I call it being human, you all.

We all have beautifully striking eyes,
Which are the windows to us without any disguise.

We laugh when happy,
We cry when sad,
So we should love one another without any regret.

We all have the same hands, and it's wonderful when someone keeps you close,
And loves you dearly, I suppose.

We all have deliciously beautiful lips to kiss someone—
The kiss that sparks everything in us, above and beyond.

Let's leave a permanent stamp in our heart—
The stamp of harmony, love, and forgiveness,
Let's make a wise choice and be smart.

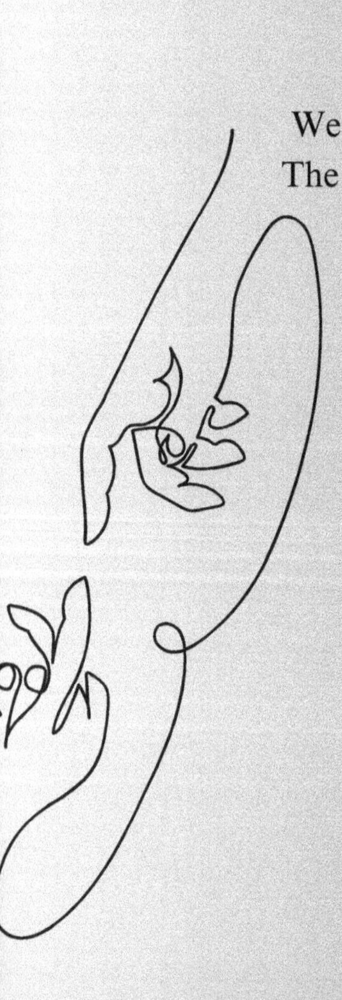

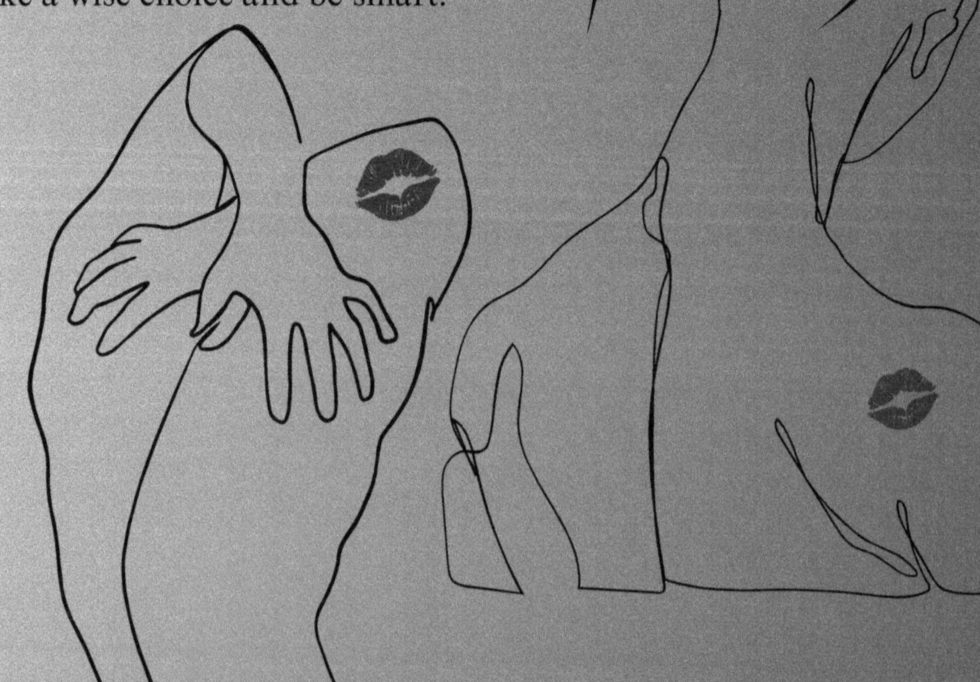

Timer

Open your eyes, wake up.
See this world and how beautiful it is without any makeup.
Put your hands up in the air,
And celebrate that you can breathe fresh air.

Look up—
Don't you wish you could fly?
Look at the birds that soar so high,
Don't you wish you could have wings,
And be one with the sky?

Celebrate yourself today.
Don't you see you have one more day?
One more day to enjoy and grow,
And leave behind every pain and sorrow.

Imagine our universe, how it grows.
Don't waste any minute, hour, or day,
Please hurry and absorb its call,
Because someday it will vanish for all.

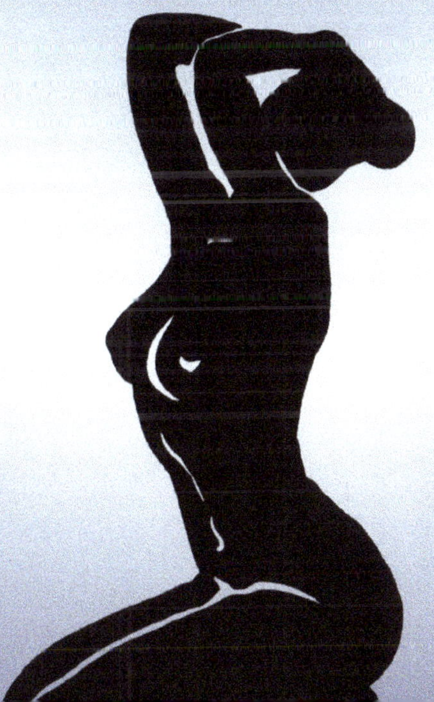

You're Finally Home

Let me relish your day,
With a kiss that is long in delay.

Let me patch up all of your pain,
Let me hug you under the magical rain.

Let me show you a new horizon,
And be the only witness to all of your
happiness that will have risen.

Let me nourish your soul,
So your spirit will be blooming and not
teary at all.

Let me pick you up,
Let me lift you up.

Let me swallow all of your regrets, sins
and mistakes,
I'd like to show you the world where love
and harmony awakes.

Please don't run away from me,
Run towards me,
And I'll greet you with the warmest hug,
I'll wipe your precious tears, just like
that.

Keeper

Let me water you with dazzling
words,
Let me shower you with delicious
desserts.

You are a queen in my book,
I will stand on my knee,
And plead you to be beside me.

I fancy for you to nourish me with
your presence,
Because your beauty is of
an essence.

Light Me Up

You and I, no matter what.
You and I always see eye to eye.
You and I would never lie.
You and I would never die.
You and I always shine.

The love we share
Is beautiful and very rare.

The words we speak to one another
Are always filled with passion towards each other.

Your gaze is outstanding,
And I don't need anyone—beside me, standing.

You are everything to me,
Even when we disagree.
You are the light that represents this world,
You are the one I need when it's awfully cold.

Focus

I will concentrate on my tomorrows.
I'm determined to forget yesterday's sorrows.

My tomorrow will be filled with love and courage.
My spirit will definitely be encouraged.

My mind won't believe in boundaries—
Boundaries that are limiting me
To be the best version of me.

I choose to be strong.
I'll figure out a lot on my own.

Seep

I want to see beyond this world,
I want to feel how everything is
Wonderful and swirled.

The beauty of a flying butterfly,
And the sound of a bird that's soaring so hig

The soothing sound of a summer wind,
The flowing river with the ocean hint.

The mesmerizing, and fluffy cloud,
With a baby blue color in the background.

The sound of a honey bee—
I wonder, without it, where would we be?
The process of pollination
Deserves a complete admiration.

The magic of each morning,
Where you can see a sunrise
And try to memorize—
Because the signature of that day
Might not repeat itself same way.

Imprint

I saw you last night,
And felt the shimmer of the mighty darkness
All over me—something I can't describe.

I looked up,
And couldn't even count all the stars up in the sky.
You looked at me and said
That you preferred my beauty in your mindset.

You said, "I love you" more than once—
It gave me wings to fly,
I felt like an angel in the sky.

You hugged me tight,
The way I always wanted you to,
I felt your cosmic energy right through.

The warmth in your voice
Gave me a memory
That leaves me no choice,
But to love you forever and feel your presence in my soul,
Even if things get out of control.

Revival

I miss you like a flower
misses the rain.

I miss you like the morning sky
misses sunshine.
I miss you like the night sky
mourns its stars
that shine so bright.

I miss you so dearly,
When your presence isn't nearly.
I miss you everyday,
Because your existence is my holiday.

Reach My Love

Be grateful everyday,
Even if it's a bit gray.

See this world with your eyes and soul,
Grab your happiness,
And remain in control.

Find your extraordinary horizons,
Let your spirit be bold,
And never let it grow old.

Walk with courage towards your tomorrows—
Like a warrior with no fear or sorrows.

Step Up

Look at today's world,
How it is broken and cold.
Look how people suffer and cry,
Because of a limitless crime.

Each one of us wonders—when will I die?
Perhaps to live with a pain and sorrow,
Is the biggest crime of your solo.

We all think that there is a white heaven and dark hell,
But what if our earth is the biggest example of hell?
The pain we endure and swallow—
If you think about it, is not too shallow.

I hope we can learn to live,
With a hope of a some day biggest relief.
I hope that our body and soul,
Will meet their creator for the sake of all.

I hope our physical and spiritual eyes soon shall be open—
Because that way, all hell will be broken!!!

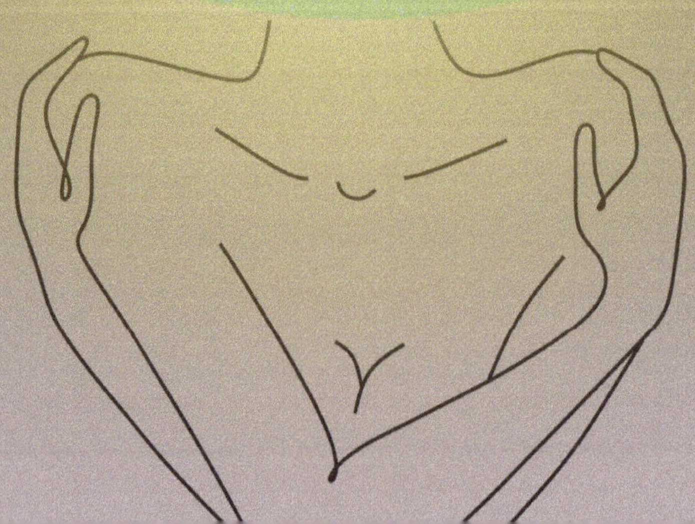

Breathe While You Can

I want to go to a place,
Where everything will be forgiven and erased.
The place that I belong to,
The place that I've been drawn to.

The place where skies are always blue,
The sun is shining no matter what I do.
The place where oceans are beautiful and calm,
Always promising there will be no storm.

The place where music's playing everywhere,
And flowers are amazing, with a hint of glare.
Where love and kindness are so near,
You can almost touch it and hear.
Where hate and anger will have no place,
With their desires and ear that requires.

This place is where your soul can grow,
Because everything negative will be let go.

God's Touch

Somewhere deep inside, each one of us holds the greatest treasure,
A place we go for comfort and pleasure—
The pleasure of being kind,
And to forgive someone who lies to ease their mind.

Our soul is our biggest gift of all,
Our soul is what connects us as a whole.
Our soul is made out of pure gold,
So it will never grow old.

We are sensitive human beings;
We'd like to be touched
With warm words and such.

We'd like to be kissed with passion,
And looked at with a gaze of compassion.
Yes, our soul is a present from our Creator,
Whose face I'd like to touch,
And eyes I'd love to watch.

I'm humbled by His gifts—
Like love, forgiveness, and hope, standing tall,
I sure would love to meet Him for the sake of all.
I'd like to ask Him so much,
All important questions and such.
I'd like to know why He created me...
Perhaps some hidden wonder still awaits me?

The Journey

There is a place for you and me,
After we die, that's where we'll be.

Imagine fields of exquisite flowers,
And every color never repeats or follows.
Colors a unique mess that devours,
They are gentle to the touch,
Offering you a wonderful aroma and such.

Imagine rivers with a flowing gold,
With our reflection that won't get old.

We'll take a boat and start to sail,
To where our love would never fail.
We'd be kind to one another,
Our kiss will mean the world to each other.

On our way, we'll pass astounding cities,
With flying angels all around.

You'll take my hand,
Asking me to go there with you
Until the very end.

The city we would end up, is built on love,
Harmony, and care,
So precisely everywhere.

We wouldn't have to talk to one another,
For without words, we'd understand each other.

The love in our hearts would never end,
Each other's company a complete godsend.

The love we'd feel would only grow,
Because there's nowhere we'd rather go.

The city we'll end up calling ours,
Will be an array of sunlight and extraordinary flowers.
There will be music everywhere,
Birds singing songs up in the air.
You'll take my hand,
And I'll take yours.

We will be dressed in shimmering white,

There will be glow,
Everywhere we go.

The air will have a scent of kindness,
There will be tears of joy.

And not a second or minute,
Of disappointment or regret—
Because we'll learn to cherish all of that.

I want to be in your garden of love,
I want to exist because you are enough.

ELENA ZUBANOV emigrated from Russia to the U.S. at twenty years old. For a while, she was able to study the English language at Rockford University. Initially, she went to school back home for fashion design. Life, however, led her down a different path. Today, she is a mother of two who enjoys creating new recipes, indulging in her love of music, and admiring the beauty of nature, particularly through horseback riding. Elena is now focused on publishing her second poetry book, as she explores new themes of her spirituality and overall purpose for being. For her, poetry and prose have become the sole motivators of living an interesting and fulfilling life, not just existing.

KRISTINA PUZIN is currently a student at Columbia College Chicago, where she is pursuing visual and dramatic arts. She has been performing as a vocalist for many years and is also an aspiring actress. At present, she is working on her first EP and gaining experience on film sets. Kristina is honored to have contributed to her mother's first book as the graphic designer, bringing Elena's visions to life. For her, success in the arts is about being innovative, and she loves discovering where the different paths lead her, whether as a musician or filmmaker.

They are each other's biggest supporters.

"Care about who you are today,
don't dwell on what happened yesterday.
Please don't forget that life is preciously delicious,
so learn to see that each moment
is absolutely nutritious."

—Elena

The door is open for you.

Take a chancc.

Walk through.

See what awaits you

on the other side.

www.ingramcontent.com/pod-product-compliance
Lightning Source LLC
Chambersburg PA
CBHW041818110726
48006CB00019B/2422